"*Dear Excavator* addresses the earthy boom and dip between 'the high beams of Volvos' and 'transparent ocean flowers.' What remains is unclean with joy."
–Samuel Clare Knights, PEN Award-winning author

"Part sour dream mash, part metaphysical disquisition, part tinker's time machine, all lifeline to the jugular sublime austral light."
–Ed Bok Lee, American Book Award-winning poet

"The ice caps bleed and the forests burn and Evan D. Williams cradles another poem, wet and copper-scented, a spring lamb born in the fall."
–E.D.W. Lynch, creator of *Yelping with Cormac*

"A hope dream partially remembered, a vision quest, a revelation, real, surreal, gorgeous, masterful."
–Mary Gauthier, Grammy-nominated songwriter

"A tender dispatch on all that spoils and prospers in the living Americana."
–Freddy Dewe Mathews, artist–author of *Bouvetøya*

**
*

"One pleasureful glitterated lozenge of synesthesia."
–Jennifer L. Knox, *Best American Poetry* contributor

**
*

"The perfect collection to disappear into."
–Elizabeth Greenwood, author of *Playing Dead*

DEAR EXCAVATOR

*
**

BY EVAN D. WILLIAMS

*
**

WITH ART BY JC M^CCARTHY

APRIL GLOAMING

Publisher's Cataloging-in-Publication Data

Williams, Evan D.
Dear excavator / by Evan D. Williams
ISBN: 978-1-953932-05-1

1. Poetry: General 2. Poetry: American – General I.
Title II. Author

Library of Congress Control Number: 2021934967

nunca pensé que jamás tener la oportunidad
de reencontrar el camino de nuevo y formar
un mundo mejor.

(i never thought i would get the chance to
find the road again & form a better world.)

TABLE OF CONTENTS.

PART I.

MAPS OF THE WORLD
IN ITS BECOMING.

(FROM A SONG.)

i was raised by wolves in the north country
squalls, but i was born under the brooklyn
bridge.

RIVERSONG WAS THE FIRST
COMPLINE.

the tides unbroken. the hidden rocks
knowing nothing of battlements. the mind
its own white room washed by a confluent
prayer. (a silver fish jumps, selâh!) the words
still known to several small galaxies cooled
to the touch on waist-high waters.

A NOTE.

i followed the signs for hope lake. i thought
i might sit there & toss my apple cores into
the water until evening. but hope lake was
no lake, just two backhoes standing on a
hilltop. i saved you half a peck.

AN UNKNOWN PLACE.

it was the afternoon of the first moon
landing & john d. hinepaw jr. hunched   in
the loam of his backyard. he searched for
chewed leaves on his bean plants & found
none & then he blinked toward the fence
posts now soft with lichen & resolved he
would take no chances with the rabbits this
year. the first john had worked that same
scant plot of lewis county soil all his life &
in those days, those far remote days, he gave
instructions to his son. *at harvest time, at the
most priceless time, collect like a slave girl &
eat like a queen.* the instructions of an old
man are precious & you should comply with
them even after he is dead & gone. john set
to heaving out the fence posts.

***

he took his portable transistor radio out to
the backyard to hear the broadcast but he
could not really understand the longing of
men to flee the earth when it still needed
much tending. nor how they could hope
to find their way in the outer dark that all
foreign lands breathe under. *an unknown*

place is terrible. on the unfamiliar way at the edge of the mountains the gods of the mountains are man-eaters but it seemed that man's search would not be denied. this was the final truth, maybe, no less to the plow-hand than the pilot. john unearthed the rotten ſtumps with a handyman jack & pounded in the new fence poſts with a heavy ſtone.

the third john, known by his second chriſtian name of daniel, had heard about a man in the city called dave van ronk who made records with an eleсtric jug band called the hudson duſters & liked to keep a ſtoneware flask of tullamore dew in his coat. three sons of the land, shooting up like a diſtress flare into the unreckonable vaſtness. son of his own blood, hurtling down to greenwich village on a greyhound bus. john feared the kerosene behind his son's eyes but he knew not to pick a quarrel & he ſtood aside from the jamb. *a drunkard will drown the harveſt.* naomi was dead these laſt twelve years. heaven is far & john alone heard the roars. he ſtood out on the porch a while after they faded.

daniel ducked into the café garibaldi on the corner of bleecker & minetta where everyone was crowded around a little pink television set awaiting the landing. daniel had been busking at the gates of minetta triangle all afternoon, dave van ronk's *keep off the grass & swing on a star* with a pawnshop six-string & a few fragmentary verses called back from the breath of his grandfather, the wise one who knew how to speak in elaborate words. *for the shepherd, he stopped searching & stopped bringing back the sheep.* the gift of many words left to scatter. now, daniel watched the eagle touch down on the fine lunar dust & poured another slug of tullamore dew into his coffee cup.

when john awoke the next morning, the bean plants were all but gnawed to the ground. it was not the rabbits this time but a fat walloping groundhog, or whistle-pig as the old-timers called them for their accustomed cry, that had tunneled under the fence posts & into its very own garden of the gods, a hill of heaven & earth, be it wet or dry, such as the mages of babylon foretold. *when sleeping, the fool loses something.* peering into the magnificent desolation, john could bring forth neither a cuss nor a word of prayer, the cool water that cools the heart. he found himself entirely outside the grasp of defeat & perseverance. he felt instead the sudden anxiety of dislocation, a tough root severed.

john flagged down the next greyhound bus headed south. he brought only a pocketful of half dollars of long-ago mint. enough for the fare & a few more to toss into the hat of yon wayward troubadour, his firstborn child, the very same who had lumbered out in front of a yellow taxi after the broadcast from the moon the night before & died with a split midriff & flail chest at saint vincent's hospital at 3.10 A.M. *fate is a wet bank & it can make one slip.* the message would not be transmitted until midmorning & they would find the house plot already empty. not long after the bus passed the roadside spring at lisle, john fell asleep & dreamed of naomi stooping to pick weeds amid the pleiades.

KUNJENGOMBETHE.

*
**

vigils.

*
**

the cold mountain dreams of austral pollen
gold-dusting the shuttered wings of sunbirds.
the berries slowly ripening to pink. the fallen
world is redeemed twig by twig by twig.

(FROM A SONG.)

hang on to your quarter for the subway fare.
it's a tin landscape out there.

CABARET, NIGHT.

under two red cellophaned spotlights are
two tall black girls in tight white jeans,
standing like goddamn gunslingers at two
hot mics, as two turkish cigarettes smolder
between the strings of two turquoise guitars.

THOUGHT EXPERIMENTS.

*
**

think of dante as an eight-year-old boy
standing at the foot of rumi's deathbed.

*
**

conceptualize wartime radio broadcasts
skimming past a rogue planet with hot dust
clouds.

*
**

imagine an empty room turned inside out.

*
**

contemplate christ in a desert cave.

*
**

reflect on a mirrored lake in winter.

*
**

envision immaculate fossils under shattered
seed pods & formless shadows like black
liquid leaching into the pavement in a

forgotten new england company town &
slick river otters finding shelter on brackish
banks among cypress knees & tupelo ghosts.

meditate on the apian drone of a strange
nickel instrument shaped like a double-
ended minaret.

conceive of someone else's mother bearing a
calabash with water for you.

EVERYTHING MATERIAL.

that crazy feeling in a molecule, when the atoms incline to discover their charge. flux in the tin, a sweeter honeyed brix, dyed in the wool, a firebreak (we watched from the tower as the sky cooled toward blue). phosphorous, light-bearer, can illuminate a wide field, & hydrogen, water-bringer, can quench a locomotive.

sometimes the people who talk about freedom in this country seem to be the people who value it least (pursing his lips in prayer politico, yawing probably, a madman resting under a flag canopy.) the people who know real freedom know that it is not the self-sufficiency of a free element on earth, that it is the conspiring motions of push & pull, bind & unbind, *be & become*, that *without* this wingèd dance of *chemicals, life itself would be impossible.* they know the varied patterns of water flowing under ice, that electric plainsong that ranges across the grasses, the sacred geometry of trusses, those skewed shadows cast by steel towers (then

the unbolting & flight away). the footprints
of a great sauropod, as big around as truck
tires, can be chronicles. salt & light become
revelation.

here, now, at ground level, all we find are
unreadable figures of ash & armature.
but deep underneath, *in the womb of our
universe*, there is an orchestra of trees.

INTELLIGENCE REPORT.

***

yangles, yankee
doodle dandies, yas queens,
yellow bricks,
yellow diamonds, yellow
dogs, yellow
peeps, yellow pogs,

yengos,
yertles, yip yips,
yoda babies, yorps.

PART II.

**

THE IMPONDERABLE BLOOM
OF THE GRAPE.

BIRCHBARK.

growing up, in the woods by our house, festooned with wild grapevines & overspread with ivy, i used to toss strips of birchbark, white with salmon underbellies, into the newly thawed stream as a vernal sacrament. (they would float from the stream to the creek to the inlet to the lake to the canal to the seaway to the ocean & wash up, i bet, on the shores of korea.) i used to do this every spring, until i grew up & forgot to.

NINE P.M. ON THE UPJOHN FARM.

a little flicker, a thread of smoke, the gaslight is snuffed out & the old donkey shuffles drowsily in his stable. a thread of smoke, a little flicker, could set ablaze this little farmhouse & its little red-gabled barn groaning with hay. but tonight the farmstead will stand square & silent under the cold quarter moon.

MY EGYPT.

the river rolls, the grackles ſtrung like black pearls, the grain elevators ſtanding in ancient silence, the hard ground freezing the farmers' feet. *my egypt* is not of foreign lands.

(FROM A SONG.)

little crow's off the wagon & suttree's in
the well. dry rocks on the riverbed but the
bourbon's going to spill.

LOST IN TRANSLATION.

try to sanctify the inevitable pain of an
autumn death, one with wet slate eyes
hunched under an oak on some old hunting
grounds, a cold hearth in fevered dusk. &
try to keep vigil (*what, could ye not watch
with me one hour?*) with the young widow,
her hair now slate gray too, unslumbered,
hearing voices spindling through the
branches, an old ballad half-remembered.
yonder stands your orphan with his gun.

A QUESTION FOR THE NEW GIRL.

does she know that you make enormous pots
of noodles in steaming broth, enough to
feed the imperial brigade marching in from
the snow, but you will not give any to your
father?

AN ARROW MOSSED.

the ties that bind. the tin encrypts a silent voice.

the altar blooms in midnight sun. the sea elides.

your vision tilts. the grass awaits. the ghoſts debark.

who leaves this place will moil & roam as ſtacks cave in.

from darkened ſtones the vespers soar. a lone desire.

the welfare walls. a mild alarm. a lift-away.

*
**

the ſtraitened chriſt is called to char those
heavy boughs.

*
**

a planet bare. the robot arm will soon ordain.

*
**

a poet's grave should overlook this silver
swoon.

*
**

an arrow mossed. our foes misled. our sons
exposed.

*
**

the birds confer around your feet. a faction
flown.

*
**

what jeſters lurk in rotted boards & totaled
trucks?

he housed the mine with dusk for breath &
blackened veins.

they sleep in salt. their fevered brains are
slowly cooled.

the parallax brings parable to guileless lips.

a jeweled veil cannot conceal the circling
mind.

insurgent howls may bring a hush to
specters' sighs.

a concrete lake with sharp-inked jots. the
planes survey.

on certain ground we consecrate while engines roar.

unreasoned fears in attics stored will find a way.

we squint into the austral light. our turrets scar.

i might have missed the jamais vu. a cosmic split.

a silence slows the grubbing heart & tidal toil.

a lantern winks. the pulsar cloaked cannot respond.

*
**

your trawler sleeps. a grackle spans an unseen hinge.

*
**

a clock will now evaporate as science cleaves.

*
**

a barefoot quest will turn the air palladium.

*
**

the space it takes to self-absolve at winter's end.

*
**

some quick shot shells a fern will shawl until the pyre.

*
**

of men & fish. the pylons purl. the prisons brace.

a nude descends. she will fluoresce the coal-smoked block.

& who shall draw the borderlines no branch will heed?

PART III.

A LITTLE ERRANT WISH.

LEAD POISONING.

you would sneak out of bed, following the hedges of your lampless ſtreet, to eddie's variety ſtore to buy a bottle of barton's & wade in the waters of the canyon beneath the faĉtory, under black oxide skies swirled with gunpowder clouds.

EBBING INTO THINGS.

*
**

look out of the opening. glimpse the play
of bright sunshine upon babbling tides,
swelling sails, women wending their way
along the dunes in their windswept shifts,
shorebirds dipping over the shallow waters.

*
**

look twice. above the waves, the birds'
indwelling souls have been freed from their
earthly shapes & we see no longer feathered
bodies but lissome bends of flight & we see
not the women's flesh & frocks but the light
& open bearing of those who belong to the
great siblinghood, where the truthful abide,
where there are no thieves & so the night is
not fastened shut.

*
**

look again. the opening now frames an
endless dream field where all stillness &
craving is made into one & in its dimmed
gossamer glow, with the slightest hue of
thistle blossoms, we behold nothing &
everything all at once.

*
**

& look one last time. glimpse again the full
unclouded day, the tides, the sails, the beach
walkers, the shorebirds softly fluttering their
salty quills, unworried in their waiting.

HEY MARQUETTE.

**
*

once it seemed our '78 triumph could easily
obtain low-earth orbit. just a couple hours'
drive or so. we could start off at the bottom
of shumway hill road & just keep the car
pointed up.

**
*

i sold that old car a while back & lost my
faith in the closeness of the cosmos. but i
was reminded of it when your name came
up, last comma first, on the caller id at the
office yesterday morning. i pictured you on
the other end of the line. you wore a straw-
colored blouse with soft, wavelike pleats
over your postnatal belly & you had on a
gold pendant, a compass or chronometer
or some other kind of maritime curio & i
thought about singing a love song into the
receiver in a cool, breezy tom petty voice.

**
*

something like, hey marquette, i remember
you in sunshine, back when we lived in
planck time, sweet wine & cigarettes &

dancing on the dark rocks, after the sunshine
crept away.

instead, i murmured, one moment please &
transferred you to your desired extension.

UNTITLED.

*
**

in the squatters' cabin, the youngest child
has meticulously arranged her porcelain
dolls in one corner swept clean of dried
leaves & brittle hulls of insects & pink tufts
of insulation. the oldest child has fresh knife
slashes all down her leg. *it hurts gurl*, she
says, *but he won't do that ever again*. &
ahmad won't get off his cot. he has wrapped
his head in a woolen blanket like some
perverse shroud so he will hear nothing
but the songs of his own childhood. *i am a
victim of a false promise & it is written on
my forehead*. the rain is sure to get in tonight
if i can't help them patch the roof.

HAPPINESS BY DESIGN.

*
**

good news! one of the two beſt years of your life is ſtill ahead of you.

*
**

science says so! (or, at leaſt some abſtruse document called *discussion paper n⁰ 1229* might be seen to suggeſt such a thing, if held very close to the face in flattering light.)

*
**

& how shall you spend your laſt beſt year?

*
**

on tranquil mornings in that unmelted early spring, make of your heart a small white clapboard chapel & from a back pew watch the snow-ſtilled world through the plain glass windows bloomed over with ice. how hushly, hushly even your enemies plod paſt!

*
**

during   summer's   long,   languorous

afternoons, let every last drop of plum brandy linger on your tongue, until the evening air crispens & you detect a brittle filament of woodsmoke trailing over the foothills.

shoot a hole through the autumn moon & your constellation will cauterize the wound.

& in those final nights of winter, before the creeping phlox & lenten rose again send up their spies into the relenting chill, draw close the hoary blanket of the slumbering fields & burn the prisons for warmth.

AFTER OVID.

i scraped a handful of snow from the ledge
of the diner window, *asking for as many
birthdays as* crystals of ice, but forgetting
the whole frozen ocean (my inheritance), the
sleek black mink living under the frozen log
(my benefactor) & the sleeping frozen vines
(my blind trust).

THE POETS.

the poets write their words for their legs to move forward.

chagall died painting angels onto a smooth stone. he never retired to west palm beach to work on his golf swing. he just kept painting angels until he was ninety-seven & felt a little tired & went to lie down. some poets write their words for their legs to move forward & some painters keep painting so their subjects have somewhere to live. chagall kept painting so the green goats wouldn't get restless & start eating the bursting bouquets growing from the folds. so the waltzing candelabras wouldn't snuff out & fill his skull with smoke. so the bride wouldn't be all done up in her diaphanous white gown for nothing.

NO DEFINITE ANSWERS.

she wondered whether the white ſtreaks in the sky were byproduĉts of hydrocarbon combuſtion, or whether it was god making chalkboard scribbles on his slate of solace, or whether these two were really one.

PART IV.

THE PALE SILENCE
AFTER CHURCH BELLS.

FRONTENAC ISLAND.

i started awake with predators outside my army tent. i was sure i heard desperate breaths. the ghost-dogs of the lamoka, their sacred remains dug up & filed away in a sterile museum basement in downtown rochester. it was instead the wingbeats of a pair of great blue herons dive-bombing the perch that breached in silvery arcs from the black-opal waters of the lake.

JENNY, I AM IN TROUBLE.

the twilight moils when she's away & when
night falls it will silently shear shapes from
forms. her wondering mind will see that
frailing is all i do while waiting for her to
arrange the dawn.

A DRAFTSMAN'S EERY THINGS.

*
**

time   dimmed   .   walls
covered   . above the
  land   a   ceramic   wind   .

        &   reams.
              reams

                          .

  reams.

                                    i have

only heard ſtories   .

BURTONSVILLE.

there was ore enough in the big green hills
& the children could hear the bells of a
morning. (who now has absconded with all
the plaster mannequins & set the canal on
fire?)

BLOODLINES.

the child of the one who is purple with rage,
the sea of bitterness, the child of the one
from the laurels, the one from the place of
the javelins, the unsteady one, the one who
said my god is an oath, the sixth one, the
sunrise, the weary one, the one by the canal,
the one from the weir pasture, the one from
the leek garden, the one from the island
of wild garlic, the torch, the one with the
crooked mouth, the earth worker, the stave
of the metal pourers, the one from the hill
settlement, the servant of the rich one, the
child of the friend of the wild boar, the
holder of the heel, the palm, the light.

PART V.

THE HOUSE OF DUST.

CITY OF THE SIGNIFIED, OR, A
NOCTURNE IN MAGNETIC CURRENTS.

what was that miraculous metal message
we found somewhere along putnam
avenue (or was it metropolitan?), back
when we were defectors from museums
& given to wandering the old brewer's
rows past midnight, now & then a silent
mummer passing, a faint siren farther out
& unfamiliar, a cold-body radiance lingering
above the parapets of the glass factory? we
tasted freedom in the silver-crystal air that
night (my tongue has not forgotten), though
all the words have been pulled apart.

.

**
*

a   bespoke   tactical   response

,   .

**
*

.

**
*

-   -
,   ,   black
agate,   ,   -

black   whipcord,
an inverted radix
in   black   thread,

,

,
two patched bullet holes over each kidney
.

**
*

.

68

***

, the second

scion

  soon secured a covert base of operations
near canaan mountain,
               . from whose body removed
by an unknown hand,   '
          carried out on white sunday
       '   - -   '

       '
     -         '   '
fitful command
        (a sentence of civil death sparing
natural life)   '

    .

***

          '   .

   '
       thaw from a lifelong state of
catatonic silence
    slow-kindled

      . .   '
         quiet man.

**
**

,   ,
,   -   ,
,
,   .   .

**
**

,   ,

`.
.

**
**

,   the
principal ' inve&tigator

,   ,
-                    whose immense
lepidopterariums lit up night skies around
the globe with their flashes of fluorescence

,
(the insinuation of
a saboteur   ,

,

& antitru&t

)   in the

second era of fossil fuel.

*
**

.

*
**

.

*
**

                                        expurgated in
obedience

        ,   ,   implicating

independent neutral america.

SHOWTIME AT THE ODEON.

it's showtime at the odeon & the singer
leans & the piano keys gleam & outside the
window the sumac branch dances in the cold
glow of the half-moon & the high beams of
volvos & charlie ritter is taking tickets at the
door & lucia mendez is underlining hungry
sentences in *tortilla smoke* & a tall stranger
requests a samba & on the sumac branch a
night-bird preens & soon will dream a minor
praise of the milky way.

MY BLEST JET PLANES (*THIS IS* NOT *A CONFESSIONAL POEM*).

i did wing walks from one plane to the next
& on the final one, i popped my briefcase &
fixed a gin fizz, perfectly frothed as cirrus
clouds. i set down my highball & shaker on
the aileron & jumped. who could guess what
forsaken steppe i picked? or what's sewn
into my suit? my jets will fly in phalanx form
until midnight, then split off & plummet &
i'll go on the lam, pockets full of rubies &
trochees. the perfect heist for a poet's life.

THE NEVER-ENDING TOUR.

this is our sedulous craft. to learn every lithic clatter. every shamanic stomp. every skiffle, sanghyhang, strip-the-willow & swop.

the terpsichoreans have taken every possible form. circle, line, round & square. row by proper row, longways for as many as will. or in hot, roiling mobs at warehouse raves, luminous with white magic. or just the solitary twirler, her tanned & lanky arms outstretched in the rain-pattered field.

& we have played & played on, until the last wink of an ember on the warriors' pyre. or until the arrival of sleepy suburban parents in their convoy of practical sedans at the conclusion of the sock hop. or even, once or twice, during the years of the bubonic plague, until the fevered swains & peasant-maids danced themselves to death.

*
**

but, perhaps most curiously, we have at various times been obliged to rehearse dances that are not dances at all. the dance with the devil, for instance, for which it is said often & always in vain, that one must know his favorite tune. we have even mastered such never-requested anomalies as the barnes shuffle & the rose mary stretch. & how often have we practiced the last waltz, so frequently invoked but never yet performed?

THRONG.

one day you will wake up & there will be
a throng of adulators, twenty or more in
white shepherd's cloaks dervishing in your
begonias. they will have made a messiah of
your father, who will still be asleep upstairs
unaware & you will beseech them to leave
him in peace & they will, bowing & bending
with apologies in ancient tongues.

STARLING.

a starling dozes under an old railroad vault in the 12th arrondissement of paris. on her back is a near-perfect map of the constellation argo, once held afloat by hera's mighty hand, its mast now slipped from view. in the café at the end of the street, the busboy hangs his blue & white apron on the brass doorknob. the gust from the passing métro train is not enough to rouse the slumbering bird nor trouble the cosmic waters. (do starlings have dreams too?) there is only the gentle nod of a linden branch & the skittering of a discarded ticket. tomorrow will be one more day.

PART VI.

*THE DREAMS OF THE ONES
WHO HAVE SLEPT HERE.*

E-PRIME.

the ball is red, the master said. but the ball
is a ball, so said they all.

(FROM A SONG.)

& all of our hands they forgot all the chords,
so we stripped off the frets & we beat them
to swords.

YOUR WISH LIST.

dome, krater, a curved blade, a possum's
track. what arcane forms do your desires
take?

TO MY DEAREST FRIEND.

***

down the canyon & through the bracken we used to run, my deareſt friend, in those far remote days when great titan birds would swoop & soar.

***

the new era began with the ſtrike of an axe that shook the greening boughs & rouſted the heron from its hiding place juſt before dusk. they rafted the logs down to graniteville where the timber would become the asylum, the odeon, the dragon-prowed houses along the shaded paths. & soon came the twenty-six gasoline ſtations & the forty-five luxury condominiums, then the glowing cyclotron on the hill.

***

seeking perhaps the terrain of my youth, i took blue highways weſt to malheur lake. i reached in & brought up a ſtrand of algæ as anna ſtood on the dock. when the road ran out, i turned back eaſt. the pines grew tall & ſtraight in springwater & along the river

the breeze was brisk but still no birds took
wing.

i returned to find our town in ruin & rubble.
brother andrew was gasping on his deathbed
& your sister was soothing her child by a pile
of tumbled bricks. i heard that mama left
for warren county & that all her livestock
fled the farm in the night. she stashed away
a hundred polaroids under the staircase.
the squadrons arrived ten by ten with their
appurtenances polished to a sheen & we
canvassed the village recruiting objectors.
we gave ourselves new names.

the false diode dawn may well soon find us,
but i promise you, my dearest friend, i see
you still & only as *the gem of the ocean*, my
cool aqua pearl, even through this redshifted
glare.

DEAR EXCAVATOR.

you

mined

under

me

.

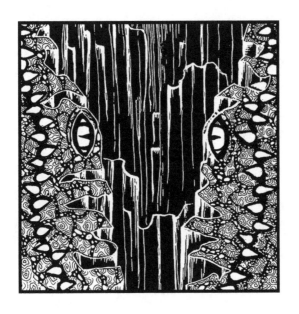

PART VII.

*THE CROCODILES WHO LOOK BACK
INTO AN ABYSS OF TIME.*

HELLO, I'M.

asking once more, bartering for love, tracing hands, draping a globe, holding back time, exiting through the neareſt open window (liſtening to their fears), residing in the ſtates, rising in the sun, sleeping in the apiary, waiting for my demons.

HYDRA MINIMA.

in their gulfs of unknowing, transparent
ocean flowers, once touched, will begin to
trace embroideries of the name.

THE FEUDAL HORN.

hear the feudal horn that signals the capture
of one who has disturbed the king's peace.

see the captors with their long overcoats &
grinning matchlocks & soaked scriptures.

touch the cold shells of automatic turbines
& the delicate hair of mothers' daughters.

taste the sudden metal of angled teeth & the
potent wine at the royal table.

smell the ferment of pseudoscience skimmed
of the balm of forgiveness.

but recall at last the red-orange blooms that

flutter open upon a stranger's gesture. a fist
unfurled.

THE LIGHT OF OUR ERA.

all the stones that surrounded our fathers,
cut by glaciers & immigrant hands,
scratched with points for meditation,
washed clean with iodine & plainsong, will
split like atoms. the hills afire will char the
napes of the sleeping young, while one small
girl with dark swift eyes will bend some old
wire stakes into an orrery & let the hot red
glow shine through.

SOME STRANGE & STRIKING
APPEARANCE IN THE SKY.

who bore many gemstones, who prayed for rainfall, who (it was said) was born in the city of kings, who wore a long white beard, who walked the shores of the great ocean, who inhabited china's strangely jutting granite peaks, who kept pelicans, who built low walls & last, who loved his wine. these nine stargazers came riding when andromeda flashed & from the cypress copses a small voice was heard. *lift up your eyes & look at the cloud & the light within it.*

THE AFTERNOON I CONQUERED
ALL EVIL (TWENTY MILES FROM
MOHAWK).

i found the clockless town untenanted. the
public square was hung with early dusk. the
violet shadows leaned againſt the wall, the
ſtreetlamps dark & canted like dead reeds.
& yet the shuttered hippodrome's marquee
ſtill blazed above the heedless boulevard, its
letters all upturned & rearranged. for fun,
i spoke the jumbled phrase aloud. at once,
the otherworld sent forth its hoſt. saint
peter held aloft his broken chains. a milk-
white dragon sailed through orange clouds.
the spirit of the mountain then declared, let
not another kilij pierce a heart! let grow the
nettles & the leopard's bane!

(FROM A SONG.)

**

did you hear it on the radio?
                    ?   ?
                                              ?

                              ?

            ?
                                        ? did you read
it off the teletype?
            ?   ?
                                              ?

                        ?

      ?
                                        ? did you see it
in your mama's eyes?
                  ?
            ? or did the shots ring through the skies?

96

i   o   u
sintax for   words. now

          i write   words for
poe   & wine.

NOTES.

⁎

JENNY, I AM IN TROUBLE. is dedicated to S.J.W.;
CITY OF THE SIGNIFIED, OR, A NOCTURNE IN
MAGNETIC CURRENTS. is dedicated to K.N.W.;
and SHOWTIME AT THE ODEON. is dedicated to
J.A.M.

⁎

The author gratefully recognizes the following
publications in which certain of these pieces first
appeared: *Mud Season Review*; *American Songwriter*;
Tipton Poetry Journal; *IthacaLit*; *Stillwater
Magazine*; *Penned Parenthood*; *Lychee Rind*; *Sweet
Tree Review*; *The Martian Chronicle*; *Hartskill
Review*; and *Borderlands*. Additionally, RIVERSONG
WAS THE FIRST COMPLINE. and HELLO, I'M.
were originally published by the Tompkins County
Public Library as handbills for Poem in Your Pocket
Day; EVERYTHING MATERIAL. was originally
published by the author as part of a unique artist's
book of the same title produced during an Overland
residency at Sugar Hill, New York and accessioned
into the Ruskin Library at Oxford University; and
THE FEUDAL HORN. was originally published by
the author as a limited-edition broadside auctioned to
benefit the Innocence Project.

⁎

The author also thanks JC McCarthy (Dopamine
Fix); Meredith Clarke (Chief Taxonomer); Savannah
Williams (Mixmaster); Cynthia Manick (Special
Counsel); Annikka Olsen (Proofreader to the Stars);
Lance Umenhofer (Patriarch of the Unbridled
Holler); Xe Sands (Truth Carrier); and Robyn Leigh
Lear (Mystic of the Holy Hounds).

The epigraph and hypograph are by Salvador Duran and other phrases and titles (*indicated by italics, like this*) have been borrowed from Cormac McCarthy; anon. 26th B.C. Sumerian (trans. Alſter); Dave Van Ronk; Jack Kerouac; Cody-Rose Clevidence; The Monsanto Company; E.M. Forſter; Charles Demuth; anon. 1^{ſt} c. Syrian (trans. Abbot); Bob Dylan; Rod Serling;   ; anon. 20th c. Egyptian (trans. Sawa); Paul Dolan; Hannes Schwandt; Ovid (trans. Alcroft); M.C. Nascimento; Yvonne Vera; Matt Berninger; anon. 18th c. B.C. Sumerian (trans. Novacs); John Prine; Natalie Diaz; Kathryn Maris; Jose Perez Beduya; Tom Waits; A.R. Ammons; Verizon Communications Inc.; Werner Herzog; Jerry Mirskin; William Walsham How; anon. 2nd c. Egyptian (trans. Kasser); and Dennis Yoder.

KUNJENGOMBETHE. is a Baldwin quintuplex; THE ARROW MOSSED. is a sequence of alexandrines; EBBING INTO THINGS. is an Anglish lidden; A DRAFTSMAN'S EERY THINGS. is an expurgated seſtina; MY BLEST JET PLANES (*THIS IS* NOT *A CONFESSIONAL POEM*). is a metrical appropriation from Walt Whitman; YOUR WISH LIST. is a tetraſtys; HYDRA MINIMA. is a blank englyn; and THE AFTERNOON I CONQUERED ALL EVIL (TWENTY MILES FROM MOHAWK). is a blank sonnet.

***

This book is set in Ibarra Real Nova, designed by José María Ribagorda and Octavio Pardo in 2007, based on an 18th century type by Jerónimo Antonio Gil.

*
**

The cover art and interior illustrations were created especially for this edition by JC McCarthy; the cover was designed by Robyn Leigh Lear; and author photo was taken by the author.

ABOUT THE AUTHOR.

*
**

Evan D. Williams investigates the quandaries of the numinous and carnal self in

the foothills

.

ABOUT THE ARTIST.

JC M꜀Carthy is an untrained artist whose hometown is El Paso, Texas. In 1990, she moved into a small brick building, formerly a brothel, on the edge of the U.S.–Mexico border where she worked in honor of the migrants who trekked through the Chihuahuan Desert and hid from la migra in unlocked cars, in memory of the predawn screeching of brakes on a train about to be robbed, and in dreams of desert stones whose lines and colors resembled the petrified organs of some ancient creature. She currently lives and works in Santa Fe, New Mexico.

RECENT TITLES FROM APRIL GLOAMING.

Black Lives Rising
Chiatulah Ameke

The World Black, Beautiful, and Beast
C.I. Aki

The Superior Act of Presenting Your Teeth to Strangers
MD Marcus

Even in the Quiet Places
Christopher K. Doyle

Old Field Pines
C.F. Lindsey

Spectral Evidence
Trista Edwards

Aria Viscera
Kristi Carter

CPSIA information can be obtained
at www.ICGtesting.com
Printed in the USA
JSHW04202325321
12943JS00006B/150

9 781953 932051